Pete Seeger

The People's Singer

by John Briggs

Atombank Books

Published by Atombank Books, Guilderland, NY

Edited by New Author Editing, Scotia, NY

Cover Photo: Colorized version of *Pete Seeger, American Folk Singer* by Fred Palumbo, 1955, *World Telegram*. Smithsonian Institution, part of the New York World-Telegram & Sun Collection.

Back Cover Photo: *Pete Seeger, noted folk singer entertaining at the opening of the Washington labor canteen, sponsored by the United Federal Labor Canteen, sponsored by the Federal Workers of American, Congress of Industrial Organizations (CIO)* by Joseph A. Horne, United States Office of War Information, Library of Congress, February, 1944

ISBN 978-0-9905160-7-1

Library of Congress Control Number: 2015947182
Atombank Books, Guilderland, NY

Biography: Pete Seeger, The People's Singer by John Briggs. The life of folk singer and civil rights activist Pete Seeger (1919-2014). Performing Arts.

To Johnny K and Pete Seeger fans of all ages

TABLE OF CONTENTS

SINGING WITH THE PEOPLE

On November 15, 1969, Pete Seeger stood in front of half-a-million people about to sing a song he had never sung before. Fortunately, Pete had a trick up his sleeve—he wasn't going to sing alone.

All those people gathered in Washington, D.C., that day to demand that the United States government stop fighting the Vietnam War. Many of these protesters were teenagers who feared they might be sent to fight. Others thought all wars were wrong. Now they stood together on a Saturday afternoon as part of the largest anti-war rally in American history.

A few days before the rally, Pete heard a woman sing a brand new song called *Give Peace a Chance.*

Pete didn't really like the song, but he believed it would make a great sing-along. He spent the next few days practicing the song to get it right.

Pete carried his banjo on stage in front of the largest crowd he had ever seen. It stretched as far as the eye could see, surrounding the Lincoln Memorial. Pete was nervous, but he calmed down as soon as he started singing. Everyone knew the song! Pete encouraged them to keep singing as other musical acts like Peter, Paul & Mary and TV star Mitch Miller jumped on stage to join in. For ten minutes, the audience swayed back and forth and sang, "All we are saying is give peace a chance."

The war went on for another six years, but Pete's performance served as the greatest moment of that peace rally. He didn't sing to his audience, he sang with them. He made them join in and feel like they could make a difference and bring the war to an end.

Not all of Pete's concerts were in front of big crowds. In fact, some of his favorite shows were in tiny places. During World War II, Pete served in the United States Army. In 1942, he and several soldiers formed a band. One afternoon, they wanted to practice. Unfortunately, they couldn't find an empty building where they could play. Finally, one of them found the perfect place: the soldiers' bathroom!

Before they finished their first song, dozens of soldiers crammed inside that bathroom just to hear them. Soon, forty soldiers were singing old folk songs like *Wabash Cannonball*. Pete and the band played for several hours, until an officer squeezed into the bathroom and ordered them to stop. It was 11:30 at night, and he wanted to sleep! Pete said it was some of the best music he ever made, and it gave him a new idea—audiences shouldn't just listen, they should be part of the show. He thought music was the best way to bring people together because everyone loves a good song.

Pete didn't know it yet, but that day changed his life. He was about to become the people's singer. Whether performing for forty people or half a million, he could always get audiences to sing along because the music wasn't his—it belonged to everyone.

EARLY LIFE

Pete Seeger was born on May 3, 1919, in New York City. His parents, Charles Seeger, Jr., and Constance de Clyver Edson, taught music. His father composed songs on the piano, and his mother played violin. When Pete was just eighteen months old, his parents packed up their luggage and instruments and took off to play classical music for people living in small towns in the southern United States. Pete's father built a special wooden trailer to carry their belongings, then put Pete, his six-year-old brother Charles III, and four-year-old brother John in the backseat of the family car. In November, 1920, the Seegers began their musical tour of the mountains.

Charles and Constance enjoyed performing in one small town after another, but after many of their concerts, local musicians would ask Charles if he wanted to hear them play. It only took a few performances for Charles to realize that these banjo players and fiddlers were some of the best musicians he had ever heard. He fell in love with American folk music.

The rest of the trip, however, wasn't much fun. The Seegers' Model T Ford could only go twenty-five miles per hour (about forty kilometers per hour), and most of the country roads were bumpy and unpaved. It took days to travel between towns. The family sometimes slept in the car and ate meals by the side of the road. Pete's mother even had to wash his diapers in boiling water over a fire. After a few months, Constance wanted to go home. Charles reluctantly

The Seeger family in 1921.
Charles is holding baby Pete.

agreed and took a teaching job at the Institute for Musical Art back in New York City.

> Pete's mother also taught at the Institute for Musical Art. Today, it's called The Juilliard School—one of the top music schools in the world!

Pete's mother hoped her children would learn to play instruments like her, but Charles III and John didn't want to. So, Constance tried extra hard to convince Pete. She left musical instruments all over the house hoping he would learn to play one of them, but Pete didn't—he learned to play all of them! At four years old, he played the recorder, the accordion, the marimba, and the piano. Still too young to read music, Pete learned by copying his parents. No matter what they played, Pete would give it a try.

Soon, however, young Pete had to leave home. His parents wanted him to get a good education. They sent four-year-old Pete to a private boarding school in Connecticut. This meant he had to live at school. He only came home for school breaks and summer vacation. Most children might have been scared, but Pete discovered that he loved being in

A 1920 Model T Ford

the country and exploring the woods near the schoolyard. He hoped to someday live in the woods like the Native Americans he read about. Pete liked the school, and so did his parents—until they learned that school officials hid the fact that Pete had gotten sick. Scarlet fever turned Pete's face and tongue bright red and left a white ring around his mouth. Although easily cured today, scarlet fever killed many children in 1925. Scared that their son could have died, they brought Pete home and never sent him back to that school.

Six-year-old Pete was happy to be home. He and his older brothers played games together and sang folk songs around the dinner table, but the good times didn't last long. Pete's parents were always fighting, and by the time he turned seven years old, his parents divorced. Charles III, John, and Pete went to live with their father, but he soon sent them to another boarding school in Connecticut.

Despite all this moving around, Pete continued to love music. When he received a ukulele for his eighth birthday, he rushed to learn new songs. Pete's mother may have gotten him interested in music, but his father recognized his talent. He gave Pete music lessons, just like he did his students. And although Pete's mother lived more than an hour away, whenever he saw her, they talked about music. She was thrilled that one of her sons loved music as much as she did, even if he didn't play the violin.

Pete's life underwent several big changes when he was twelve. First, his father met Ruth Crawford, a songwriter who collected and wrote folk songs. Charles and Ruth loved playing those old tunes together, and they married in November, 1931. Although Pete still lived much of the year at boarding school, at home he now had a stepmother who encouraged his interest in folk music.

The following year, Pete changed boarding schools again. Pete was an average student, getting mostly B's and C's, but he was a star when it came to school activities. During his second year at Avon Old Farms, Pete started his own school newspaper because he

Charles Seeger sometime before 1945

Ruth Crawford Seeger sometime in the 1940s

thought the official school paper was boring. Always looking for a good story, he interviewed students, teachers, and people in town. Pete charged a nickel for the *Avon Weekly Newspaper* and often sold every copy. After a few months, though, he wanted to stop. That's when the headmaster called Pete into his office and told him he couldn't quit.

"Why?" asked Pete, who thought it was his

newspaper and he could quit whenever he wanted.

The headmaster told him that a very wealthy woman liked his newspaper more than the school paper. Since she gave the school a lot of money, Pete printed a new edition every week to keep her happy.

He did this until he graduated two years later. Besides earning some extra money, Pete said he learned a very important lesson: never be afraid to ask a stranger a question.

Not surprisingly, Pete's best school activity was music. He used to practice on his teacher's banjo, but didn't like asking him to use it all the time. When he was thirteen, his music teacher took him shopping for a used banjo. Pete picked through the instruments hanging on the wall until he found a beat-up banjo he liked. He then joined the school jazz band. Pete soon discovered

---

Charles Seeger's Children

With Constance de Clyver Edson

1. Charles III (born 1912)
2. John (1914)
3. Pete (1919)

With Ruth Crawford

4. Mike (1933)
5. Peggy (1935)
6. Barbara (1938)
7. Penny (1943)

---

two problems: no one wanted to practice as much as he did, and whenever he tried to dance around the stage, pieces of his old banjo fell off. Embarrassed, Pete begged his parents to buy him a much nicer banjo, and two years later, he got his wish. Pete stayed in the jazz band, though they still didn't want to practice as much as he did.

In the summer of 1935, Pete switched from jazz to his first love, folk music. His father took him to the Mountain Dance and Folk Festival in North Carolina. Pete stood mesmerized by the music of five-string banjo player Samantha Bumgarner. He said she could "ripple out a rhythm" no matter what song she played. Pete dedicated his last year at school to mastering the five-string banjo just so he could be as good as Samantha.

Although Pete had not gotten great grades in school, he still applied to go to Harvard College, perhaps the best college in the country. Pete's father could not afford to pay the $400 per year it cost to send Pete there, so Pete's older brothers paid most of the bill. What they didn't know was that Pete would get involved in something on campus that affected him for the rest of his life.

The Seeger Family

Alan Seeger

Pete Seeger could trace his American roots all the way back to the Mayflower in 1619. He claimed to be a descendant of William Brewster, the senior elder of the Pilgrims. Brewster was the only Pilgrim to have a college education, so he served as their minister. The four Brewster islands in Boston Harbor are named after him.

One of the most famous Seegers was Pete's Uncle Alan. He was one of the first Americans to die in World War I. He died on July 4, 1916, from machine gun fire. His brother's death turned Charles, Jr. into a **pacifist**. Alan wrote the poem *I Have a Rendezvous with Death* about a man who believes he is going to die young. It was one of President John F. Kennedy's favorite poems. President Kennedy also died young when he was murdered in November, 1963, while visiting Dallas, Texas.

COLLEGE & COMMUNISM

Pete was seventeen years old when he entered Harvard College in Cambridge, Massachusetts. Writing his own school newspaper convinced him to become a reporter, so he studied journalism. Pete also took art classes, where he learned to paint. He struggled in the classroom, but just like high school, Pete excelled in **extracurricular** activities.

The first group Pete joined was the American Student Union. Its members were pacifists like Pete's father, and they were dedicated to one thing: stopping Adolf Hitler and the Nazis in Germany. Although Word War II was still three years away, the American Student Union feared Hitler wanted to conquer Europe. In early 1936, the German army attacked the Rhineland, a part of Germany taken away from it after World War I. Hitler claimed he was simply taking back land that once belonged to Germany, but the American Student Union believed Hitler was starting another world war. They urged world leaders to stop Hitler before he attacked another country.

Leaders in one country agreed with the American Student Union. The Union of Soviet Socialist Republics (also known as the USSR or the Soviet Union) suggested that European countries like Great Britain and France refuse to trade with Germany. Soviet leaders hoped this would weaken Germany's economy and force Hitler out of power. The American Student Union had many communist members who supported the Soviet idea because the USSR was a communist country.

When Pete learned this, he joined the Young Communist League. This was a bold move because many Americans did not like communists. Communists believe that people should not own property, and that people should not be rich or poor. Most Americans believe in **capitalism**, or the right to own private property, like your own home, and that people will be rich or poor depending on how hard they work. For Pete, communism meant living like Native Americans. The more he studied communism, the more he liked it. As Pete said, "The Communists opposed Hitler, and I opposed Hitler. The Communists supported workers' rights, and I supported workers' rights. The Communists supported civil rights, and I supported civil rights."

Being a communist in America may have been daring, but it hardly surprised Pete's family. Pete had an uncle who took him to his first May Day parade when he was fourteen. May Day is like Labor Day in America, except people celebrate it on May 1st. Pete's father was also a communist. He hoped to secure better working conditions and more pay for factory workers, farmers, and low-income people.

May Day vs. Labor Day

More than eighty countries honor their workers on May Day. The United States celebrates Labor Day on the first Monday in September because President Grover Cleveland didn't want people to celebrate the more popular holiday, which began after eleven people died while demanding an eight-hour workday.

KARL MARX

Karl Marx (1818-1883) was a German writer who believed life was a battle between rich and poor people. He thought the upper class took advantage of the poor and did not pay them enough money. He predicted that the working classes would

Karl Marx in 1882

rise up and remove the rich from power. They would form a new government, pay workers fairly, and abolish private property.

In 1844, Marx met Friedrich Engels. They wrote about the lives of working people. The Union of Soviet Socialist Republics became the first communist country in the world in 1919. In 1989, its economy collapsed. Today, there are only a few communist countries left.

Karl Marx died in London, England. His theories go by different names, including Marxism, communism, and socialism.

*The Haymarket Affair in Chicago, Illinois, on May 4, 1886.
Seven police officers and four protesters died when the
workers' rights rally turned violent.*

All these activities hurt Pete's grades. He was close
to flunking out. When Pete learned his brothers were
running out of money, he knew it was time to leave
Harvard. In the fall of 1938, nineteen-year-old Pete
quit school before he finished his sophomore year.

Out of school and out of work, Pete had to find a
way to make money. His Aunt Elizabeth, principal
at the Dalton School in New York City, offered him
a job teaching folk music to high-school students.
Pete gladly accepted the job, but it didn't pay very
much. He traded paintings for food and a place to

sleep. Unfortunately, when the school year ended, so did the job.

To make money, Pete joined The **Vagabond** Puppeteers. They spent the summer of 1938 performing puppet shows for farmers and their families in upstate New York. To save money, the group didn't eat in restaurants or sleep in hotels. Farmers fed them at every show and let them stay in their homes. On nights when they didn't have a show, they cooked food over a fire and slept under the stars. Pete was living just like his family did when he was a baby. He was too young to remember it then, but he loved it now.

Many of The Vagabond Puppeteers shows were at union meetings. A union is a group of workers who get together to improve their pay and working conditions. The farmers in upstate New York formed a union so they could get more money for their milk. In August, 1939, 14,000 farmers voted to stop delivering milk to bottling plants. The farmers worried that their strike would fail, however, because they didn't believe city workers would support them. To their surprise, city workers in unions backed their strike and wouldn't buy milk until the price went up. The strike was a big success, and Pete realized that people everywhere, no matter how different they seemed, could get along if they just talked to one another.

When fall came, Pete was out of work again, until he received an offer from family friend Alan Lomax. Alan asked Pete to work at the Library of Congress in Washington, DC. Charles, Jr. had moved to the nation's capital the year before to collect folk music from all over the country. Both men knew how much Pete loved folk music and thought he would be perfect for the job. Not only did Pete help them collect and organize thousands of songs, he learned to play some of them on his banjo. Alan encouraged Pete to keep practicing and learn every song he could.

A Dairy Farmers Union meeting in August, 1939

A few months later, Pete received an offer to perform in California. An actor named Will Geer was putting on a benefit concert for struggling farmers. Pete immediately hopped on a train to travel across the country. The concert took place on March 3, 1940, a day Alan Lomax called "the beginning of modern folk music."

It was the day Pete Seeger met Woody Guthrie, the most famous folk singer in America.

Woody Guthrie

Woody Guthrie was born in Oklahoma in 1912. He wrote more than one thousand folk songs and influenced dozens of folk singers who tried to copy his style. In the 1930s, Guthrie was a radio star, but he liked performing live more than anything. His most famous song is *This Land Is Your Land*, which reminds people that the United States is a country for everyone, not just the rich and powerful. He died in 1967, just as his son, Arlo, was becoming a famous folk musician, too.

Like Pete, Woody hated Adolf Hitler and the Nazis. Written on his guitar was "This Machine Kills **Fascists**" (fash-ists) because the Nazis were fascists!

PETE & WOODY TEAM UP

Pete and Woody instantly liked each other when they met in 1940. Woody was seven years older than Pete and a terrific songwriter. Pete thought Woody could teach him to write better songs, and Woody liked the way Pete played his banjo. After the concert, they went their separate ways, but knew that someday they'd play together again.

Pete spent the spring and summer of 1940 traveling the country, playing the songs he learned at the Library of Congress. Audiences in New England admired his banjo brand of folk music as much as they did in the South, and soon Pete was performing regularly. When Alan Lomax found out what a good musician Pete had become, he invited him to appear on his radio show, *Back Where I Came From*. Plenty of the country's best folk singers, including Woody Guthrie, Lead Belly, and Burl Ives, appeared on the show, which aired three times a week on CBS. The show was popular, but it wasn't making any money. Companies refused to advertise on the show because it was **integrated**. This meant that black and white musicians performed together. Companies were afraid that if they advertised on the show, white people in the South would not buy their products since the South was **segregated**. This meant that white and black people could not go to the same places or even be friends. Companies wouldn't even advertise on a special show for soldiers that Alan taped at the White House. Unable to make money on the program, CBS canceled it in February, 1941.

Pete now spent his time putting together a songbook for union workers called *Hard Hitting Songs for Hard-Hit People*. While looking for someone to publish his book, Pete heard that a man named Lee Hays was working on a book for union workers, too. Pete tracked Lee down to make sure they weren't using the same songs. After all, he didn't want them to write the same book! In less than a month, Pete and Lee were performing together. Lee

A segregated water fountain in 1938

had a deep voice that sounded good next to Pete's banjo. Millard Lampell, Lee's roommate, joined the group, and they soon sold hundreds of tickets a week for twenty-five cents apiece.

One day, Lee said the group needed a name. He felt every good musical group had to have a name. Pete spotted the word **almanac** in the songbook he'd written. Lee liked that word. He said in his home state of Arkansas, "Farmers only have two books: the *Bible* and *The Farmers' Almanac*." He suggested they call themselves The Almanac Singers, and the name stuck.

The first thing The Almanac Singers did was make

Pete in the middle of The Almanac Singers

a record. They filled *Songs for John Doe* with anti-war songs urging the United States not to fight in World War II. This was not unusual for an American in 1941. Although the war had been raging in Europe since 1939, eighty percent of Americans wanted to stay out of the war. Famous Americans like pilot Charles Lindbergh and carmaker Henry Ford said the war was not an American fight but a European one. President Roosevelt, however, believed the United States would one day enter the war and wanted Americans to be ready. When he heard the album, he asked if the government could stop stores from selling it. Archibald MacLeish, the head of the Library of Congress, said that would be against the law because the group had a right to its opinion. Roosevelt didn't like that answer, but said, "Well, at least no one will hear it." He was right. Few people bought the record, though it sold enough copies in communist bookstores to encourage The Almanac Singers to make a second record.

Their next record contained the kind of music Pete and Lee knew best: songs about working people. Pete insisted they include Woody's song *Union Maid**. The song about a poor woman who couldn't be scared away from joining a union became a big hit with union members. When The Almanac Singers performed it in front of 20,000 people at New York City's Madison Square Garden, everyone sang along. After the concert, Pete contacted Woody and asked him to join the group. "Everybody knows your song," Pete told him. By the time Woody reached New York, The Almanac Singers were getting ready to travel across the country to perform at union rallies. Woody decided that since he'd come all this

Hear all songs marked * at *johnbriggsbooks.net*!

way to join them, he might as well go on the road, too.

The group bought a giant, 7-seat automobile. They played everywhere they could, from factories to shipyards to union meetings. Just like in New York, everybody loved Woody's song, but Pete and Lee were struggling to get along.

Pete let anybody who wanted to play join The Almanac Singers on stage, but Lee wanted the band to be a small, professional group of musicians. Unhappy with Pete's approach, Lee claimed he had throat problems and couldn't sing anymore, so he went home to New York. A few weeks later, Millard left the group, too. Pete and Woody finished the tour, but didn't know if the band would stay together because they faced a much bigger problem. A few weeks before their tour started, Germany attacked the

Who Was Pete Bowers?

Communists were so unpopular that Pete didn't use his real name with The Almanac Singers. He called himself Pete Bowers because he didn't want to hurt his father's career in the U.S. government!

Woody and Pete performing together

Soviet Union. Suddenly, capitalist countries like the United States and the United Kingdom sided with communist countries to stop Hitler. In late 1941, Pete started going to Communist Party meetings again, something he had not done since college. Although communists were still not popular in America, they were more popular than Nazis.

Six months later, on December 7, 1941, Japan attacked the United States at the Pearl Harbor Naval Shipyard in Hawaii. The surprise attack sank eight battleships, destroyed 188 airplanes, and killed more than 2,000 sailors. The very next day, America declared war on Japan and its allies, including Germany. President Roosevelt called the attack on Pearl Harbor "a date which will live in **infamy**." Pete quickly signed up for the military draft. Now supporting the war, The Almanac Singers released an album of pro-war songs called *Dear Mr. President*. The record featured another Woody Guthrie song that became famous, *The Sinking of the Reuben James*, about the first American ship sunk in the war. But a song by Woody, Pete, and Millard became their big hit. You could hear *Round and Round Hitler's Grave** all over the radio. CBS invited the group to appear on its stations twice. Decca Records, one of the biggest record companies in the country, wanted The Almanac Singers to work for them. The William Morris Agency, a powerful talent agency in Hollywood, wanted to help the group get more work. The Almanac Singers were hot!

Round and Round Hitler's Grave included lyrics like this:

I wish I had a bushel
I wish I had a peck
I wish I had a rope to tie
Around old Hitler's neck

Yikes! People were mad at Adolf Hitler for starting World War II, and this song captured it perfectly.

Then the problems started. Newspapers reported that The Almanac Singers were communists. CBS,

Decca, and William Morris quickly dropped them. Communists were now America's allies, but a lot of people still didn't trust them. Among the people who didn't trust communists were agents at the FBI. Unable to prove that The Almanac Singers were communist spies, the FBI smashed every copy of *Songs for John Doe* they could find so that people couldn't hear it.

All those problems, however, were about to be put to rest. In July, 1942, eight months after the attack on Pearl Harbor, Pete got his orders to join the Army. The Almanac Singers broke up because one of its leaders was going to war.

A PACIFIST GOES TO WAR

Pete reported for duty on July 17, 1942, and the Army promptly sent him to Keesler Army Airfield in blistering hot Biloxi, Mississippi. Private Pete Seeger grabbed his banjo, a few personal items, and set off to become an airplane mechanic. Pete's grades were so good, though, that his training officer recommended he join the Army Corps (Core) of Engineers. That was dangerous work. Engineers didn't stay behind like airplane mechanics—they served in combat, building roads and bridges so soldiers and tanks could attack the enemy. Sometimes they blew up roads and bridges, too. Despite the danger, Pete agreed to become an engineer because he still wanted to stop the Nazis.

On the day Pete was supposed to take the engineers test, he got sick. The Army rescheduled the test for him, but he never got to take it. A stern officer called him into his office and bluntly asked, "Are you a Communist?" Pete said yes, and the Army confined him to base. Although the United States and the Soviet Union were now allies against Germany, the Army didn't want communists in its ranks.

World War II

World War II was the biggest war ever fought. It lasted from 1939-1945 and saw twenty-one million people die. The two sides were divided into the Allied and Axis powers.

Allies	Axis
The United Kingdom	Germany
The United States	Italy
The USSR	Japan
France	Four other countries
Canada	
Eighteen other countries	

The Army started reading Pete's mail, looking for any sign that he might be a spy. Pete wasn't, and so the Army let him stay on base, play his banjo, and read books to pass the time. After ten months, the Army let him leave, but he wasn't going to war. They gave Pete fifteen days to go home and marry his girlfriend.

Pete and Toshi Ota met a year and a half earlier at a square dance in New York City. When it was over, Toshi asked Pete to walk her home. He jumped at the chance to spend time with her. They discovered they had more in common than square dancing. Both liked art, volunteer work, and supporting civil rights. Seven months later, in June, 1942, Pete took Toshi to Washington, DC, to meet his father. He surprised everyone (including Toshi!) by announcing they were getting married.

Of course, the Army had different plans. They delayed Pete's **furlough** for a month before letting him go home to marry Toshi. Toshi rushed to put together a small wedding at a church in New York City. She and Pete had so little money that Toshi had to borrow her grandmother's wedding ring to put on her finger. They had two weeks together before Pete went back to Mississippi.

On the base, Pete hung around the barracks and

Toshi and Pete's wedding photo

played his banjo, occasionally getting a pass to leave the base for a few days. During this time, he taped a music special for British radio and made two records, but Pete felt like he was not involved in the war effort. After eleven months, the Army gave Pete new orders: ship out—and take your banjo with you.

In June, 1944, Pete boarded a steel-gray Navy cruiser and set sail for Pearl Harbor. For four weeks, Pete staged a variety show, singing songs and acting in short comedy sketches for the soldiers and sailors. He then played three times a week for wounded soldiers at the local Red Cross hospital. Pete came to believe that if he couldn't fight fascists in Europe, he could at least raise troop **morale** at home. And

Pete performing in Washington, DC, for soldiers and First Lady Eleanor Roosevelt

he figured the best way to do that was with fast-paced and **jaunty** folk songs that often kept his audiences whooping and hollering and singing out loud.

Several months later, Pete got the best news he could imagine: Toshi gave birth to a baby boy, Peter Ota Seeger. Pete was so excited that he let out a holler of his own and pinned the message to his locker so he could remember his son back home. He couldn't wait to travel 5,000 miles back to New York and hold his newborn son. Unfortunately, Peter, whom everyone called Pitou, was very sick. He had seizures and couldn't digest food. After six months of struggling, baby Peter died. It devastated Pete that he never saw his son and could not comfort his crying wife.

In September, 1945, World War II came to an end, and Corporal Pete Seeger, like millions of other soldiers, headed home. He was determined to start a family with Toshi and continue his music career. Pete planned to form a singing labor movement willing to fight for working-class people. Pete had a new war to wage—he just didn't realize how big it would be.

NUMBER ONE ON THE
HIT PARADE

Pete didn't waste any time getting to work after he came home from the war. He and Toshi started a family right away and had two children—Daniel and Mika—in three years. On the musical side, Pete appeared in the 1946 short film, *To Hear Your Banjo Play*, with Woody Guthrie, and performed in elementary schools whenever he could. He hoped working with children would help him write a book called *How to Play the 5-String Banjo*. He and Lee Hays also launched *The People's Song Bulletin*, a folk music newsletter that published labor songs. Unfortunately, many unions were arguing over whether to be communist or anti-communist. Pete couldn't bring the two sides together and stopped publishing the magazine when many workers stopped buying it. At least this time he didn't have to keep writing to make a wealthy woman happy!

For most people, that might be enough, but for Pete, it was just the beginning. In 1948, he supported presidential candidate Henry Wallace. Wallace wasn't a Republican or Democrat—he was part of a new political party called the Progressive Party. Pete liked that Wallace supported equal rights for all people. He also liked that Wallace wanted a friendly relationship with the Soviet Union so that the two sides wouldn't go to war. Pete performed at the Progressive Party's convention in 1948 when Wallace became the official candidate for president. It was late July in steamy Philadelphia, but supporters happily joined Pete in singing, "The donkey and the elephant go 'round and 'round the merry-go-round." Pete felt Republicans (whose symbol is the elephant) and Democrats (the donkey) didn't have any new ideas for making the United States a better country.

Despite the support of thousands of people, Wallace lost the election. He let communists support him, and this made some voters hate him. Down South, people threw eggs and tomatoes at him when he tried to make speeches. Wallace finished fourth in the election. He even lost to the one candidate who supported segregation.

In 1949, Pete and Toshi left New York City. Pete and Toshi bought some land on a mountain in upstate New York so Pete could live out his dream of living in the woods. The only way to get to their log cabin—which they built themselves—was to travel along a bumpy dirt road. The cabin had no running water or electricity. Pete chopped wood to make a fire for heating and cooking, Toshi carried water from a nearby creek, and everyone had to go to the bathroom in an outhouse. Sometimes their children even slept outside on blankets under the stars. Pete thought he was living like an early pioneer; his kids felt like it was permanent camping.

Unfortunately, Pete's problems followed him to the country. He agreed to be part of a benefit concert that summer in Peekskill, New York, about twenty miles (thirty-two kilometers) from his home. The star of the show was actor Paul Robeson, a communist who sent his son to school in the Soviet Union. As Robeson and a friend drove to the concert, a radio announcer said angry protesters had gathered along the road. Some of these protesters were in the Ku Klux Klan, an organization that hates black people.

Paul Robeson

As Robeson approached, they attacked his car with rocks and baseball bats. Unable to get to the stage, Robeson canceled the show. The protesters cheered, but they had not yet scared him away.

Two weeks later, on September 4, 1949, Robeson planned another concert. While some protesters showed up, they were no match for the 20,000 people who arrived to watch the show. Concertgoers and union members locked arms and formed a human chain several miles long to keep protesters from attacking the performers. A police helicopter flew overhead looking for trouble, and union workers acted as security guards on the ground. Still, some protesters got through. As Pete's car approached—with Woody Guthrie, Lee Hays, Toshi and their two children, including baby Mika, inside—protesters threw rocks at the car. Woody hung a red shirt over a window to keep the shattered glass away while Toshi covered her children with her body. Somehow, they made it to the stage, but

Rioters in Peekskill, New York, flip over a car.

they were too scared to ever forget that day. Pete built part of his log cabin's chimney out of the rocks that landed in his car as a permanent reminder of the riot.

It's hard to believe that less than one year later, Pete would be among the biggest stars in the world.

Rioters severely beat Eugene Bullard, the first African-American combat pilot. Though captured on film, no one went to jail.

In November, 1948, Pete and Lee, along with guitarist Fred Hellerman and singer Ronnie Gilbert, formed a new band called The Weavers. They named it after a German play about a garment workers' strike in 1844. They figured that, like The Almanac Singers, the group would play at union meetings and civil rights gatherings.

The Weavers, from left to right: Pete Seeger, Ronnie Gilbert, and Lee Hays. Front Row: Fred Hellerman

One night in 1950, music producer Gordon Jenkins approached them about making a record. Decca, where Jenkins worked, said no. They didn't want the same trouble with The Weavers they had with The Almanac Singers. So, Gordon snuck The Weavers into the studio and recorded two songs. Stuck with the record, Decca released it.

Their first song, *Tzena, Tzena, Tzena***, originally written in Hebrew and translated into English, was a fast-paced and fun song that went all the way to number two on the record charts. When disc jockeys flipped the record over and played the other side, *Goodnight, Irene* exploded on the charts. The slow waltz, written by Lead Belly, remained the number one song in the country for thirteen weeks. Record stores sold two

Goodnight, Irene

million copies and *Goodnight, Irene* finished 1950 as the most popular song of the year.

See videos for all songs marked **
at *johnbriggsbooks.net*!

Sadly, Lead Belly never saw *Goodnight, Irene* become a big hit. He died six months before it was released.

It seemed like The Weavers were everywhere—on records, radio, and TV. They rushed to release more songs, from classic folk tunes like *On Top of Old Smoky* and *Darling Cory* to original numbers like *If I Had a Hammer** and *Kisses Sweeter than Wine*. One of the group's biggest hits was the first American recording of *Wimoweh***, a South African song about the great Zulu king, Shaka. Most people didn't know that *Wimoweh* got its name because Pete heard the title wrong—they just liked the music!

All of this was about to come to an end. The problem with getting good attention is that you sometimes get bad attention, too. The people who hated communists were about to strike again, only this time, it was much worse.

The Story of *Wimoweh*

South African songwriter Solomon Linda composed *Wimoweh*, or *Mbube* (Em-boo-bay) as it is called in Zulu, in the 1920s. The title means "He is a lion!" and the song's most famous words, "The lion sleeps tonight," were made up by Solomon while performing it live. Alan Lomax thought the song would be good for The Weavers, who invited Solomon to sing with them on the record. The record company claimed the song was very old and refused to pay Solomon for writing it. When Pete found out they were ripping off Solomon, he sent him $1,000 (about $10,000 today) and ordered Folkways Records to send all his future money for the song to Solomon. Folkways said they would, but never did.

Wimoweh went on to become a hit for many other singers. When Disney used the song in *The Lion King*, Solomon's family, now very poor, sued to get paid. Disney eventually gave the family $15 million dollars for the song. Solomon's family could now live like a Zulu king themselves!

THE RED SCARE

One day in the spring of 1950, a young man in his late twenties walked into the FBI office in New York City. He had a simple offer. He would spy on American communists for money.

Harvey Matusow, a part-time actor and reporter, joined the Communist Party in 1947. The FBI figured he knew a lot of communists because he worked as a clerk in a communist bookstore. They agreed to hire him, and that summer, Harvey wrote down the names of communists and what they discussed at their meetings. When his friends found out what he was up to, they kicked him out of the party. The FBI then fired Harvey since he could no longer help them catch communists.

But that didn't stop Harvey. He approached the House Un-American Activities Committee, better known as HUAC (Who-Ack). HUAC was a committee in the U.S. House of Representatives that investigated people they thought didn't like America. At the top of their list were communists. They accepted Harvey's offer to spy for them. Within two years, Harvey gave them a long list of names:

- Folk singers who worked at *People's Songs*
- Union workers, including one of their leaders
- 126 people who worked at *The New York Times* Sunday newspaper

Harvey included two famous names on his list: Pete Seeger and Lee Hays. As soon as the news broke that The Weavers had two "commies" in their midst, the band was placed on a blacklist. A blacklist is a list of people, often in show business, who are banned

---

The Red Scare

Urging people to fear communists was called "The Red Scare" because the Soviet Union's flag was bright red.

---

from working. The Weavers went from having a big hit with *Wimoweh* in 1952 to finding out that stores would no longer sell their records, radio stations would no longer play their songs, and most concert halls would no longer let them on stage. Just like Peekskill, protesters came to their few concerts and threatened fans. Unable to get work, The Weavers broke up a year later. In order to make money, Pete started teaching music in elementary schools, sometimes performing for the students. He also wrote a children's music column for *Sing Out!* magazine. He called his column *Johnny Appleseed, Jr.* because he thought children were like apple seeds that could be sprinkled around the country spreading messages of peace and fairness.

Although The Weavers were gone, trouble still followed Pete. He had to testify before HUAC. The committee questioned him in Washington, DC, on August 18, 1955, but it was hotter inside that room than out. Committee members fired lots of tough questions at Pete, yet he stayed calm and told them he would not "answer any questions as to my associations… my religious beliefs, or my political beliefs, or how I voted in the last election, or any of these private affairs. I think these are very improper questions for any American to be asked."

*Pete enters the courthouse with his guitar
slung over his shoulder.*

When Lee Hays appeared before HUAC, he
claimed the Fifth Amendment, but Pete claimed the
First. He believed he had a right to be a communist
even if the committee didn't like it. Pete was the first

First Amendment vs. Fifth Amendment

First Amendment

Have you ever heard of free speech? This comes from the First Amendment to the United States Constitution, the highest law in America. It means you have a right to your opinion, even if somebody else thinks it's wrong.

Fifth Amendment

Have you ever heard someone say, "I plead the Fifth?" This refers to the Fifth Amendment of the Constitution. It means you don't have to testify against yourself in court. You don't have to admit to a crime even if you did it. The government must prove you did something wrong. This ensures that you're "innocent until proven guilty."

person to claim the right to free speech in five years, and it made the committee members mad. When they accused Pete of being un-American for singing the song *Wasn't That a Time** (written by Lee Hays and poet Walter Lowenfels, about good times in America that were really bad), Pete said he'd play the song for them on his guitar, but that made them even madder. They thought Pete was making a joke out of the hearing. Pete said he loved America, but had different views about how things should be. His accusers didn't believe him, and a year and a half later, when Pete still refused to answer their questions, they found him in "**contempt** of Congress." Pete was not allowed to leave New York unless he told the government where he was going. Finally, in 1961, a judge sentenced him to one year in jail and a fine of up to $10,000 ($80,000 today).

Pete never served a day in jail, though. A year later, a judge threw the case out of court. It had been nine years of court battles, but he had won. Pete was a free man.

Harvey Matusow was not.

In 1952, Harvey went to work for Senator Joseph McCarthy, the toughest anti-communist of them all. Three years later, Harvey released a book called *False Witness* saying he lied to Congress. He lied when he said there were 126 communists working at *The New York Times* Sunday edition. There couldn't be because only 100 people worked on the Sunday newspaper. He lied when he said Pete was currently

Senator Joseph McCarthy (left) talks with lawyer Roy Cohn during the Army hearing, in which the senator accused the United States Army of having communists in its ranks.

a Communist. Pete stopped going to Communist meetings in 1949. Harvey also said that Senator McCarthy asked him to lie. Harvey was convicted of perjury, or lying in court, and sentenced to three years in jail. He was eventually blacklisted from working as an actor.

The Weavers, however, returned to work. Carnegie Hall in New York City defied the blacklist and asked them to perform on Christmas Eve, 1955. The concert quickly sold out. More than 2,000 people bought tickets to see them sing their best-known

Why Pete Left the Communist Party

Pete left the Communist Party because he could no longer defend Joseph Stalin, the leader of the Soviet Union. Stalin killed millions of people while in power. At first, Pete didn't realize just how brutal Stalin was, but when he learned the truth, he could no longer support him. He said he remained "a communist with a little c" because he still believed in communism, just not the Communist Party.

Pete's support for the Soviet Union in the 1930s earned him the nickname "Stalin's Songbird." He apologized for his support and continued to help working people anyway he could.

songs, including *Goodnight, Irene, Wimoweh*, and *Pay Me My Money Down*.* A year and a half later—and a month before Joe McCarthy died — *The Weavers at Carnegie Hall* became one of the best-selling folk albums of all time. Despite the "Red Scare," The Weavers were back!

Unfortunately, the good times didn't last long. Despite their success, most theaters still wouldn't book

The Weavers at Carnegie Hall

them. Desperate for money in 1958, The Weavers recorded a song for a cigarette company. Before agreeing to sing the commercial, The Weavers voted on it. Pete argued that cigarettes were bad for you and the group shouldn't promote them, but he lost the vote 3-1. Although he disagreed, Pete recorded the commercial with them. He realized that sometimes in a democracy your side loses. That doesn't mean you don't obey the idea of "majority rules." After singing the cigarette commercial, however, he left The Weavers.

Pete needed a new challenge, and he found one in the civil rights movement.

Joe McCarthy

Joseph McCarthy (1908-1957) was a senator from Wisconsin. He led the charge against communists in the late 1940s through the mid-1950s. He believed communists were trying to take over the United States, and claimed they were working for President Harry S. Truman, the U.S. Army, and the State Department. He often accused people of being communists with very little proof. These types of attacks are now known as McCarthyism.

In 1954, the Army fought back. They said McCarthy wanted them to give special treatment to one of his former aides who joined the military. The senator said the Army was trying to get revenge because he accused them of hiding communists. The public, the media, and the FBI sided with the Army. On December 2, 1954, the U.S. Senate voted to condemn Joe McCarthy's actions. His witch-hunting days were over. He died just three years later from an enlarged liver.

WE SHALL OVERCOME

In the 1950s, Pete primarily performed at schools in order to make a living. Sometimes he even recorded his concerts and released them as records. But one school proved more important than all the others.

In the summer of 1957, Pete traveled to Tennessee to celebrate the 25th anniversary of the Highlander Folk School. This school taught young people how to be leaders in the civil rights movement. While there, Pete performed the song *We Shall Overcome*. This song had the lyrics "we will overcome," but he changed the word "will" to "shall" because it was easier to sing. He also added a new verse, one that said people can find strength in one another. The verse began "We'll walk hand in hand," something people did when marching to show they were united.

The audience liked the song, but one very important person helped bring it to the rest of the world. As Dr. Martin Luther King, Jr., left the school that day, he kept humming *We Shall Overcome*. Once in the car, he turned to the person next to him and said, "Boy, that song sure sticks with you."

Within three years, *We Shall Overcome* was the anthem of the civil rights movement. Protesters sang

From left to right, Martin Luther King, Pete Seeger, Rosa Parks, and Ralph Abernathy stand next to a student at the Highlander Folk School in 1957.

it as they waited to be served in "whites only" restaurants. They sang it on college campuses and in jail cells. They sang it at folk festivals and community centers. And they sang it while marching for the right to vote in Alabama as the police moved in to beat them. Dr. King even quoted that song at his last Sunday sermon in 1968 before being murdered on a hotel balcony only two hundred miles from where he first heard it.

While people were held together by a common cause—the belief that everyone should be treated equally—Pete realized that his dream of bringing people together through music was coming true. What he didn't know was that it would get a whole lot more popular in the next ten years.

The Library of Congress declared *We Shall Overcome* the most powerful song of the 20th century.

The Origins of *We Shall Overcome*

Music historians long believed that *We Shall Overcome* began as the song *I'll Overcome Someday* (written in 1901), and versions of the song were printed in the *People's Songs Bulletin* as early as 1947. Much of the music and some of the lyrics, however, are actually based on the song *If My Jesus Wills* by the Reverend Mother Louise Shropshire, a longtime friend of Dr. King's. A folk singer named Guy Carawan sped up the song and created the version people still sing today. The 1963 March on Washington and Pete's 1963 recording of *We Shall Overcome*, taped at Carnegie Hall with the Freedom Singers, brought the song to an even bigger audience.

The Reverend Mother Louise Shropshire in 1962

A BIG, MUDDY MESS

Pete began the 1950s as a popular performer, but he began the 1960s as a popular songwriter. A few of the thousands of children Pete had performed for were now recording his songs or buying them. The Kingston Trio, a group Pete said was "barely out of high school," released *Wimoweh* and the anti-war song *Where Have All the Flowers Gone?*, while Peter, Paul and Mary had a top ten hit in 1962 with *If I Had a Hammer*. But no one did better than a group called The Byrds. They topped the charts in 1965 with *Turn! Turn! Turn (To Everything There Is a Season)*, which Pete wrote using words from the *Bible*.

Pete even managed to get in one hit of his own. In

1964, he released *Little Boxes*, written by his friend Malvina Reynolds. The song wasn't a big hit in the United States, but it went all the way to number one in Australia. The song encouraged listeners to be original thinkers, or, as we say today, "to think outside the box." The song was so popular that Australian musicians opened up dozens of folk clubs and invited Pete to tour the country. Audiences liked Pete's version so much that whenever Malvina tried to sing it, people told her she was doing it wrong—they liked Pete's version better!

Joan Baez and Bob Dylan, two regular performers at the Newport Folk Festival

The Newport Folk Festival

In 1959, Pete co-founded the Newport Folk Festival. Many future stars got their big breaks here, including Joan Baez and Bob Dylan. Country music superstar Johnny Cash and Pete became good friends at the festival because Johnny, who was part Cherokee, was impressed by how much Pete knew about Native American history.

The most famous story about the festival came in 1965 when Bob Dylan played rock 'n' roll instead of folk music. According to the legend, Pete ran backstage with an ax to cut the wires so Bob couldn't play his electric guitar anymore. The true story is that Pete ran backstage all right—to turn down the guitar because people couldn't hear the words to the song *Maggie's Farm*. When the sound engineer refused, saying, "That's the way they want it," Pete said, "If I had an ax, I'd cut the cable right now."

Pete might not have liked Bob's new music, but it made Bob Dylan one of the most successful songwriters of the past fifty years.

Pete's musical success at last led him back to television. The blacklist kept him off big TV shows like *The Ed Sullivan Show* and *The Tonight Show*, but when ABC banned Pete from appearing on *Hootenanny*, which only invited folk musicians on the air, Pete had had enough. He and Toshi approached a small station in Newark, New Jersey, with an idea for a folk music show. *Rainbow Quest* aired thirty-nine episodes in 1965-1966. Many famous musicians appeared on the show as a favor to Pete, including Johnny Cash and Tom Paxton. And like the Newport Folk Festival, many future stars got their big break here. It was a small step, but Pete felt he was at last breaking through the blacklist.

Unfortunately, it took a war and two brave comedians to fully get Pete off that list.

As the Vietnam War raged on in Southeast Asia, more than twenty performers recorded *Where Have All the Flowers Gone?*, a song in which young girls pick flowers growing above the graves of dead soldiers. Considered one of the greatest political songs ever written, it captured the fears of a nation at war, much as *'Round and 'Round Hitler's Grave* captured America's anger during World War II. But it wasn't that song that finally got Pete off the blacklist.

The Smothers Brothers, a comedy duo that sang folk songs, had a popular show in the late 1960s. They asked Pete to come on their first episode of the second season in 1967, but CBS was nervous. TV executives didn't want to offend viewers or advertisers. CBS finally gave in, but only if Pete agreed to sing several songs so they could choose their favorite. Pete sang *Waist Deep in the Big Muddy*, a song in which an army captain foolishly leads his men into a deep river, where he drowns. Pete felt this was how the United States was fighting the Vietnam War—getting in deeper and deeper until the country was in over its head. Pete also sang *Where Have All the Flowers Gone?* and *Wimoweh*.

CBS aired the last two songs, but cut *Waist Deep in the Big Muddy* from the show. The Smothers Brothers quickly claimed that Pete's performance had been **censored**. Reporters accused CBS of denying Pete his First Amendment right to free speech. Then, in January, 1968, the Vietnamese Army launched the Tet Offensive, the biggest battle of the war. Although the United States eventually won the battle, it took months of hard fighting, and Americans began to believe they were losing the war. Now that the Vietnam War was extremely unpopular, CBS realized it would be good to put Pete on the air. In

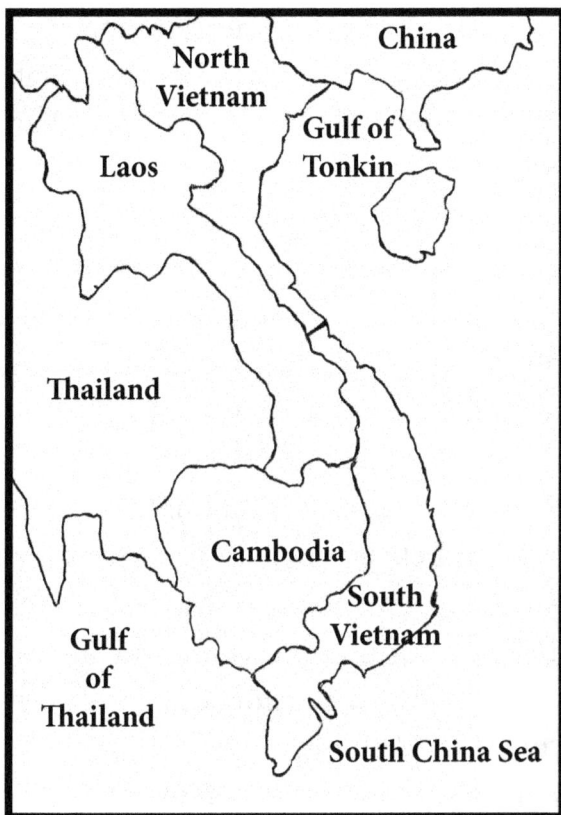

A map of Southeast Asia during the Vietnam War

In February, 1968, he finally performed *Waist Deep in the Big Muddy*** for a nationwide audience. Pete Seeger was officially off the blacklist.

A year later, Pete led 500,000 people in that famous sing-along at the Vietnam Moratorium, but his problems with the war were not over yet. In 1972, he visited North Vietnam, America's enemy, hoping to end the war. Although the United States and North Vietnam signed a peace treaty less than a year later, Pete had little to do with it, and people back home accused him of giving "aid and comfort to the enemy." They believed he was a Communist again.

When Johnny Cash invited Pete to appear on his TV show, *Johnny Cash and Friends*, two years later, the hate mail poured in. Fans wanted to know how Johnny could have someone so "un-American" on his show. Johnny asked Pete about his visit to North Vietnam, and Pete explained his reasons for going. Johnny called Pete "a great American" who just wanted peace, but that didn't end the angry letters against Pete. It took a far more dramatic event.

One night, a Vietnam veteran who saw several friends die in the war, came to one of Pete's concerts in New York's Catskill Mountains. He planned to kill Pete. When Toshi found out, she told Pete he had to talk with the man. Pete found him, and after they talked about the war, they sang *Where Have All the Flowers Gone?*. The man couldn't hold back his tears and said, "I feel clean now." He no longer wanted to kill Pete. Instead, he believed that Pete was a man of peace trying to do what he believed was right. The man struggled to forget the horrors of war, but he at last came to understand those who wanted peace. Pete found a way to make an enemy his friend.

Coretta Scott King (Martin Luther King, Jr.'s widow) at the Vietnam Moratorium

The Vietnam War (1964-1973)

The United States fought the war in Vietnam to stop the spread of Communism in Southeast Asia. The United States, South Vietnam, and Australia battled North Vietnam, a country supported by China and the Soviet Union. More than one million people died in the war, including 58,000 Americans. Although U.S. soldiers began leaving Vietnam in 1973, the fighting did not stop until 1975. It is the only war the United States ever lost, and Vietnam remains a Communist country more than forty years later.

ANOTHER BIG, MUDDY MESS

When Pete was a boy, families spent the day fishing and swimming in the Hudson River. They could spend the entire day enjoying a picnic along the banks of this scenic, 300-mile-long waterway that stretched from the Adirondack Mountains in upstate New York all the way down to New York City. But by the 1960s, the river was filthy. Factories discharged toxic waste into the water, while cities dumped in their sewage. The Hudson was a dangerous river, and it smelled awful. No one dared fish or swim in it. In fact, it was so deadly near New York City that if you fell in, people rushed to clean you off so you didn't get sick. The water was that bad.

In 1966, Pete decided it was time to clean up the Hudson River, which ran near his home in Beacon. Inspired by the Algonquians, a Native American tribe who believed they should protect the river, Pete and Toshi organized The Great Hudson River Revival to draw attention to the problem. Thousands of people showed up to hear Pete sing, but he realized one concert would never change things. They needed something big. Something people couldn't miss. Something that would draw lots of attention to the dark and dirty river.

That's when a big idea hit him: he would sail a long, sleek ship called a sloop up and down the Hudson. Boats chugged along the Hudson every day, but none of them were 106-foot, 19th-century sailboats. Curious people would ask about it and hopefully join the cause to clean up the river.

Pete and Toshi joined the search for an old sloop stored along the Hudson, hoping they could fix it up. They found a few wrecks here and there, but nothing they could make seaworthy. Having failed to scrounge up an old ship, they built a new one. Pete, Toshi, and several of their closest friends raised money to construct a brand new sloop. It took two years to get the money, but by late October, 1968, shipbuilders in Maine got to work. Roughly seven months later, the Clearwater set sail for New York City with a few folk singers on board acting as the crew. While others celebrated as the ship reached New York Harbor, Pete remained worried that they hadn't done enough. He felt the ship was just an interesting museum piece, but it wasn't doing anything to clean up the river. He

> In 1969, Pete and folk singer Tom Winslow wrote *Hey Look Yonda (It's the Clearwater)*, the first environmental song written or co-written by an African-American musician. It's still the Clearwater's theme song.

made the decision that the boat had to sail up the Hudson River all the way to the state capital in Albany to educate people about just how dirty the river was. He knew then that people would demand action.

And demand action they did. People wrote government officials and attended public meetings calling for laws to protect the river. Finally, three years later, Congress passed a clean water bill that made it illegal to dump sewage into rivers—and not

The Sloop Clearwater

just the Hudson, but every river in America.

With that battle won, Pete set his eyes on the next big problem: companies dumping billions of gallons of toxic sludge into the Hudson every year. This fight, however, wasn't so easy to win. Factories spent millions of dollars on lawyers who said that cleaning up the river was the government's job. The federal government said the companies made the mess, so they should clean it up. It took several decades of court battles and public meetings, but eventually companies like General Electric agreed to clean up the Hudson River. Pete and his Clearwater team won again!

Today, thousands of families vacation along the Hudson every year, fishing, swimming, and boating. The Environmental Protection Agency (better known as the EPA), which is in charge of making sure America's land and water are clean, gave all the credit to Pete and his organization for this amazing feat.

Every year, students learn about the Hudson River by climbing aboard the Clearwater. It's not just a museum, it's a floating classroom! The Clearwater Foundation even has a smaller ship that's also a floating classroom. It's named the Woody Guthrie, after Pete's longtime friend.

Find out how you can visit the Sloop Clearwater at Clearwater.org!

REAPING THE REWARDS

A line in Pete's song *Turn! Turn! Turn!* says there is "A time to plant, a time to reap." This means that you plant seeds early in the year, and then pick the fruits and vegetables when they're ready. Pete spent his entire life "planting seeds" by fighting for workers' rights, racial equality, free speech, peace, and a clean environment. Decades later, when some of those ideas blossomed, Pete reaped the rewards. People around the country honored him for a lifetime of great music and noble causes.

PETE'S MUSICAL HONORS

The earliest honor Pete received came in 1972. That's when he was inducted into the Songwriters Hall of Fame for the many hits he wrote, including *Guantanamera, If I Had a Hammer, Where Have All the Flowers Gone?* and *Wimoweh*. More than twenty years later, in 1996, Pete Seeger, legendary folk singer, joined the Rock & Roll Hall of Fame because so many rock stars, including The Byrds, The Tokens, Johnny Rivers, and Bruce Springsteen, recorded his songs. That's right, the man who once tried to unplug Bob Dylan for playing electric guitar was now celebrated by rock and roll fans everywhere!

Pete also won several Grammy Awards, the highest honor in the music industry. He won twice—in 1995 and 2008—for Best Traditional Folk Album, and then again in 2010 for Best Musical Album for Children. He also won a Lifetime Achievement Award from the Grammys for everything he had done in the music business. But Pete felt uncomfortable winning such awards. Instead of boasting about winning his second Best Album Grammy, Pete apologized to the other nominees because he felt they made great music, too. Of course, he may have had to apologize. One of the nominees he beat was his younger sister,

Peggy!

In 1994, The Kennedy Center for the Performing Arts in Washington, DC, named after President John F. Kennedy, honored Pete for his contribution to music and American culture. And earlier that year, President Bill Clinton invited Pete to the White House so he could give him the National Medal of Arts. In the city where Congress once tried to silence Pete and his music, the president of the United States now placed a medal around his neck.

Whenever people gave Pete an award for his music, they always mentioned his support for civil rights. Pete loved music, but he also saw it as a way to bring people together. That message finally got through.

PETE'S CIVIL RIGHTS HONORS

In 2014, the Woody Guthrie Center in Tulsa, Oklahoma, announced a new award: the Woody Guthrie Prize. They would give it to the person who tried to make sure that "this land was made for you and me." Of course, the award went to Pete for working alongside Woody to make America a place where everyone is equal.

A Single Protester

Pete liked to tell this story about the importance of sticking to your beliefs:

In 1951, a young Quaker stood in Times Square in New York City at midnight holding a sign calling for peace. A man approached him and said, "Do you really think you're going to change the world with that sign?"

And the young man said, "I suppose not, but I'm sure not going to let the world change me."

PETE'S WORK CONTINUED

All these awards didn't mean Pete forgot the world still had problems. In 1982, he performed at a benefit concert to support union dock workers on strike in Poland. The money he raised was used to help workers buy food, clothing, and other items while they stayed on strike. This was a big step for Pete. Poland was a Communist country run by the Soviet Union, and police attacked the strikers. By supporting it, Pete showed that he didn't like communism the way the Soviet Union practiced it. This strike proved to be the beginning of the end for the USSR.

Even in his eighties and nineties, Pete continued to be active in social causes. When the Iraq War started in 2003, motorists spotted Pete standing all by himself on the side of the road near his home in Beacon holding a sign calling for peace. He could often be found picking up garbage in parks to keep the environment clean. In September, 2013, Pete took the stage in Saratoga Springs, New York, as part of Farm Aid to raise money for struggling farmers just as he had done in California in the 1930s.

Pete's last concert came two months later, on November 30th. He joined Arlo Guthrie, Woody's son, for a performance at Carnegie Hall, the very place The Weavers staged their big comeback. The two of them delighted the audience with a performance of Woody's *This Land Is Your Land*. The audience cheered for an encore, so they did the song again. Although Pete had been performing for more than seventy years, audiences still loved him, and they let him know it.

The one person who had been with Pete through all the hard times, though, was not there to enjoy that night. Toshi, his wife of sixty-nine years, passed

Pete performing in 1986

away four months before. She was with Pete when rioters attacked him in Peekskill. She was with him when he walked into court to fight for his freedom. She was with him when he traveled around the globe making home movies of tribal musicians. She was with Pete whenever possible, whether in their cabin in the woods or on the road trying to save the world. Toshi was with him almost until the end.

And the end came soon. Six months after Toshi died, Pete passed away, too. The good news was that he was as active at the end of his life as he had been during it. Just ten days before he died, Pete was out chopping wood, getting ready for a cold winter night. When he fell ill, his family rushed him to the hospital, where, on January 19, 2014, Pete Seeger, a man who had toured the world and tried to change it, passed away in New York City, only one hundred blocks from where he was born ninety-four years before.

The world lost a legendary folk singer that day, but his legacy lives on.

Rock star Bruce Springsteen, who recorded an album of folk songs called *The Seeger Sessions*, said Pete beat his enemies because he outlived them.

The day before Pete died, he lost the Grammy Award for Best Spoken Word Album to talk show host Stephen Colbert. Stephen told millions of viewers that one of the greatest honors of his career was having Pete on his show.

PETE SEEGER'S LEGACY

Pete Seeger had a huge impact on the world of folk music. An entire generation of folk singers grew up listening to him sing. Alongside Woody Guthrie and Lee Hays, Pete created modern folk music, but he did far more than either of them to teach it. By being a part-time music teacher, visiting schools, appearing on *Sesame Street*, and making children's records, Pete encouraged thousands of children to sing along to his songs. When those students grew up, many of them formed folk groups of their own and kept right on playing his music. Pete's book, *How to Play the 5-String Banjo*, sold hundreds of thousands of copies and led many young people to learn the banjo. Not only did they learn to play like Pete, they sometimes learned to play on a copy of Pete's own banjo!

That's because Pete also invented his own banjo. It's called the long-neck banjo because it's longer than most banjos. Thousands of folk musicians fell in love with its sound and felt it was easier to play.

Pete was also the first to use the steel drum, from the country of Trinidad and Tobago, in folk music. Immigrants from all over the world brought their music

> *"I'd rather sing in schools than just about anyplace else."*—Pete Seeger

to America, but Pete was different—he was an American going all over the world to bring their music home. He brought *Guantanamera* from Cuba, *Tzena Tzena Tzena* from Israel, and *Wimoweh* and *Abiyoyo* from Africa. Once, while performing in the Soviet Union in 1965, Pete got the audience to sing along to *Michael, Row the Boat Ashore* even though they didn't speak English! Even the home movies he made while traveling around the world are some of the last films ever made of African people doing ancient dances.

Perhaps Pete's biggest influence was the way he

convinced today's folk singers to fight for justice. Although Woody, Lee, and Pete often worked together on civil rights, Pete stood up to others when it meant going to jail. He didn't cave in when it came to fighting Congress. He argued that his beliefs were his First Amendment right. This led hundreds of folk singers to act just like him. His courage inspired them to march for causes they believe in.

Pete's fight for justice was reflected in his life's work. His songs are among the most important political songs of his day. The magazines he founded—*The People's Songs Bulletin* and *Sing Out!* wrote about workers' rights, racism, and peace. Perhaps most importantly, Pete asked others to take a stand on their own or alongside him. He wanted everyone to make a difference in the world.

> *"I'm not sure I've made a difference, but I know one thing: when you're involved with these issues, you work with the good people."*—Pete Seeger

People have paid tribute to Pete in many different ways. In Beacon, not far from his cabin, you can enjoy the great outdoors at the Pete and Toshi Seeger Riverfront Park. It used to be a junkyard until Pete started fixing it up. Other people, including lawmakers, want bridges and roads named after him. Singer Harry Chapin, who performed with Pete at many benefit concerts, wrote the song *Old Folkie* about him. And every week, Pete's song *Newspaperman* airs as the theme song for the national radio show *The Media Project*. Some listeners say it's their favorite part of the show!

Pete Seeger never called himself a folk singer. He preferred "a singer of folk songs." But whatever kind of music he sang—new songs, old songs, fun songs, serious songs—Pete didn't like to sing alone. His ability to get his audience involved in music and the fight for justice is what made him the people's singer.

TIMELINE

1914-1917	World War I fought.
1916	Alan Seeger died at the Battle of the Somme.
1919	Pete Seeger born.
1929	The Great Depression began.
1932	Franklin D. Roosevelt elected president.

1934	Pete went to his first May Day celebration.
1935	Pete learned to play the banjo.
1936	Pete joined the Young Communist League.
1939-1945	World War II fought. The United States enters the war in 1941.
1940	The Almanac Singers formed.
June 1941	Germany attacked the USSR.
December 1941	Japan bombed Pearl Harbor.
1942	Pete drafted into the Army.
1948	The Weavers formed.
1949	Pete stopped attending Communist Party meetings

1950	*Goodnight, Irene* named the number one song of the year.
1952	The Weavers blacklisted
1953	Joseph Stalin died.
August 1955	Pete testified before the House Un-American Activities Committee.
December 1955	The Weavers performed at Carnegie Hall.
1957	Pete met Martin Luther King, Jr.
1962-1973	United States involved in the Vietnam War.
1963	Martin Luther King led the March on Washington.
1964	Pete had his only solo hit with *Little Boxes.*
1965	The Byrds hit number one with *Turn! Turn! Turn!*

1967	Pete removed from the blacklist.
1968	Martin Luther King assassinated.
May 1969	The Clearwater set sail.
November 1969	The Vietnam Moratorium held.
1972	The Clean Water Act became law.
1982	Pete supported Polish dock workers on strike.
1989	The Soviet Union collapsed.
1994	Pete received the National Medal of Arts.
1999	Pete received a Lifetime Achievement Grammy.
2014	Pete Seeger died at the age of ninety-four.
2015	The Hudson River officially clean.

HISTORICAL FIGURES

The Algonquians: A native people who lived primarily in New England and Canada, and around the Great Lakes.

The Almanac Singers (1940-1942): An influential folk singing group that sang union work songs. Its two best-known members were Woody Guthrie and Pete Seeger. The group opposed World War II until Germany attacked the Soviet Union in 1941.

William Brewster (1560-1644): The senior elder and religious leader of the Pilgrims.

Johnny Cash (1932-2003): A country music singer known as "The Man in Black." He befriended Pete at the Newport Folk Festival and later called him "a great American."

Bob Dylan (1941): A folk singer who became one of the most successful songwriters in history.

Henry Ford (1863-1947): Founder of the Ford Motor Company. He improved the way cars were made.

Will Geer (1902-1978): An actor and activist who won an Emmy Award for playing the grandfather on the TV show *The Waltons*. His concert brought Woody Guthrie and Pete Seeger together.

Woody Guthrie (1912-1967): A folk singer and radio star who wrote *This Land is Your Land*. He is the father of folk singer Arlo Guthrie.

Lee Hays (1914-1981): A folk singer and founding member of The Almanac Singers and The Weavers.

Burl Ives (1909-1995): An actor and folk singer best known for Christmas songs and for playing the snowman in *Rudolph the Red-Nosed Reindeer.*

Huddie Ledbetter (1888-1949): "The King of the 12-String Guitar" performed under the name Lead Belly (sometimes Leadbelly). He wrote the song *Goodnight, Irene.*

Charles Lindbergh (1902-1974): The first person to fly solo across the Atlantic Ocean. It took him thirty-three hours in 1927. Early on, he opposed the United States fighting in World War II.

Alan Lomax (1915-2002): A collector of traditional folk and blues songs for the Library of Congress.

John F. Kennedy (1917-1963): The 35th president of the United States and the youngest elected president in U.S. history. One of his favorite poems was I *Have a Rendezvous With Death* by Alan Seeger.

Solomon Linda (1909-1962): A South African Zulu musician who wrote *Mbube*, better known as *Wimoweh*.

Martin Luther King, Jr. (1929-1968): A civil rights leader who led the Montgomery Bus Boycott and the March on Washington. One of the most revered Americans, his birthday is now celebrated nationwide.

Archibald MacLeish (1892-1982): An award-winning poet who was in charge of the Library of Congress from 1939-1944.

Harvey Matusow (1926-2002): An American communist turned FBI and HUAC informant who later recanted his testimony.

Joseph McCarthy (1908-1957): A U.S. Senator from Wisconsin who accused people of being communists without proof. His actions were condemned by the Senate.

Paul Robeson (1898-1976): An actor and activist attacked at the Peekskill Riots in 1949. He is best known for singing *Ol' Man River*.

Franklin D. Roosevelt (1882-1945): The 32nd president of the United States, who led the country through the Great Depression and World War II.

Charles Seeger, Jr. (1886-1979): A music teacher, composer, and folk song collector. He was Pete Seeger's father.

Ruth Crawford Seeger (1901-1953): An influential composer of modern classical music who later composed folk songs.

Shaka (circa 1787-circa 1828): A powerful Zulu king and military leader who united his people in South Africa.

Louise Shropshire (1913-1993): The creator of *If My Jesus Wills*, a major influence on *We Shall Overcome*.

The Smothers Brothers: A musical-comedy team, Dick and Tommy Smothers hosted the TV show, *The Smothers Brothers Comedy Hour*. They let Pete sing *Waist Deep in the Big Muddy* for a nationwide audience.

Bruce Springsteen (1949): A rock musician known as "The Boss". He played with Pete at President Barack Obama's 2009 inauguration and released an album of Pete's songs called *The Seeger Sessions.*

Joseph Stalin (1878-1953): Leader of the Union of Soviet Socialist Republics and one of the most cruel dictators of the 20th century. He ordered millions of people put to death.

Henry Wallace (1888-1965): Former vice president of the United States who ran for president in 1948 for the Progressive Party and lost. He supported civil rights, workers' rights, and negotiating with America's enemies rather than fighting them.

The Weavers: A popular folk group whose career stalled during the Red Scare. They inspired countless young people to become folk singers.

GLOSSARY

Almanac: a book published every year that contains facts and figures

Capitalism: an economic system that encourages private property and the accumulation of money and goods

Censor: to officially block or delete something because you don't agree with it

Contempt: an extreme dislike for something or someone

Extracurricular: student activities done at school, such as sports or clubs

Fascist: a strong patriot who believes in a government that controls its people

Furlough: a vacation for soldiers

Infamy: famous for a bad reason, such as committing a crime or being mean

Integrated: mixed together

Jaunty: upbeat or lively

Morale: the feelings a person or group has about a task or duty

Pacifist: one who opposes war for any reason

Segregated: separated for being different

Vagabond: a person who wanders from place to place without a job

PHOTOGRAPHS

Page 5: Prof. Charles Seeger & Family, National Photo Company Collection (Library of Congress), May 23, 1921

Page 7: Quarter front view of Ford touring car, Library of Congress Prints and Photographs Division, 1923

Page 9: American musicologist and composer Charles (Louis) Seeger by Harris & Ewing, sometime between 1905 and 1945

Page 9: Ruth Crawford Seeger, Dio Portrait Studios, Mid-1940s

Page 12: Portrait d'Alan Seeger, History and Heritage Division Foreign Legion

Page 17: The Haymarket Riot by T. de Thulstrup, Harper's Weekly, May 15, 1886

Page 19: Dairy Farmers Union Meeting in Watertown, NY, *Watertown Daily Times*, August 10, 1939

Page 21: Woody Guthrie by Al Aumuller, *World Telegram*, March 8, 1943

Page 24: Civil Rights Segregated Water Fountain by John Vachon, 1938

Page 35: Pete Seeger, noted folk singer entertaining at the opening of the Washington labor canteen, sponsored by the United Federal Labor Canteen, sponsored by the Federal Workers of American, Congress of Industrial Organizations (CIO) by Joseph A. Horne, United States Office of War Information, Library of Congress, February, 1944

Page 40: Paul Robeson by Gordon Parks, Office of War Information, Library of Congress, June 1944

Page 41: Peekskill Riots, *The Reporter Dispatch*, September 5, 1982

Page 44: Publicity photo of Huddie Ledbetter (Lead Belly), before 1950

Page 49: Pete Seeger arrives at Fed. Court with his guitar over his shoulder by Walter Albertin, *World Telegraph*, April 4, 1961

Page 52: Sen. Joseph McCarthy chats with his attorney Roy Cohn during Senate Subcommittee hearings on the McCarthy-Army dispute, New York World-Telegram, 1954

Page 59: Louise Shropshire in Cincinnati, Ohio, January, 1963

Page 61: Civil Rights March on Washington, D.C. [Entertainment: closeup view of vocalists Joan Baez and Bob Dylan.] by Rowland Scherman, U.S. Information Agency Press and Publications Society, August 28, 1963

Page 67: Crowd of people holding candles, including African Americans, at a march at night to the White House, lead by Coretta Scott King as part of the Moratorium to End the War in Vietnam, *U.S. News & World Report*, October 15, 1969

Page 72: The sloop Clearwater sailing south on the Hudson River, *WorldIslandInfo.com*, May 28, 2006

Page 79: Pete Seeger Concert by Joseph Schwartz, February 20, 1986

Page 91: Charles Lindbergh, Harris & Ewing, Library of Congress Print & Photographs Division, 1915-1937

Page 93: Franklin Delano Roosevelt by Elias Goldensky, Library of Congress, December 27, 1933

And see plenty of Pete Seeger videos at
johnbriggsbooks.net!

REFERENCE MATERIALS
Books

Cohen, Ronald D. and Capaldi, James (Edited by). (2014). The Pete Seeger Reader. Oxford University Press

Dunway, David King. (2008). *How Can I Keep From Singing: The Ballad of Pete Seeger*. Villard Books: New York, NY

Seeger, Pete. Rob Rosenthal and Sam Rosenthal (Edited by). (2012). *Pete Seeger in His Own Words*. Paradigm Publishers: Boulder, CO

Newspapers

The New York Times. *Harvey Matusow, 75, an Anti-Communist Informer, Dies* by Douglas Martin. February 4, 2002

The New York Times. 1948: *Live... From Philadelphia... It's the National Conventions* by Reuven Frank. April17,1988

Poughkeepsie Journal. *Seeger Introduced King to 'We Shall Overcome' in 1957* by John W. Barry. January 31, 2011

The Reporter Dispatch, *Peekskill's Day of Infamy: The Robeson Riots of 1949* by Steve Courtney. September 5, 1982

Websites

FanPal.com. *Pete Seeger*

The Journal for MultiMedia History, Volume 1, Number 1, *The 1939 Dairy Farmers Union Strike in Huevelton and Canton, New York: The Story in Words and Pictures.* Fall, 1998

State of the Planet, The Earth Institute, Columbia University, *Seeger's Legacy Lives on Aboard Sloop Clearwater* by Amy McDermott. May 13, 2014

Suite Io. *Fifteen Facts About Pete Seeger* by Craig Sanders

WoodyGuthrie.de. *The Almanac Singers*

Radio

WAMC, Northeast Public Radio. *Pete Seeger: A Life*. Interviewed by Dr. Alan Chartock. March, 2001.

Films

Pete Seeger: The Power of Song. (2007). Directed by Jim Brown. Jim Brown Productions

ALSO FROM

ATOMBANK'S

BIG BIOGRAPHY SERIES

MARY DYER, FRIEND OF FREEDOM

JUDY GARLAND: LITTLE WOMAN, BIG TALENT

UPCOMING BOOKS

JIM THORPE, ATHLETE OF THE CENTURY

LOOK FOR THEM AT

ATOMBANKBOOKS.COM!